Cover image by   Kaisa Ullsvik Miller
Author photo by   Jed Miller

Published in the United States by   Fence Books
                                        New Library 320
                                        University at Albany
                                        1400 Washington Avenue
                                        Albany, NY 12222
                                        www.fenceportal.org

Book design by   Rebecca Wolff

Fence Books are distributed by   University Press of New England
                                        www.upne.com

and printed in Canada by   Westcan Printing Group
                                        www.westcanpg.com

Library of Congress Cataloguing in Publication Data
        Ullsvik Miller, Kaisa [1978–]
        Unspoiled Air/ Kaisa Ullsvik Miller

Library of Congress Control Number: 2008920756

ISBN 1-934200-12-3
ISBN 13: 978-1-934200-12-4

FIRST EDITION

The author wishes to express her gratitude to the Daily OM for words that spread stillness, laughter, and encouragement. And to Jed for the same.

Fence Books are published in partnership with the University at Albany and the New York State Writers Institute

and with generous support from the above and from the New York State Council on the Arts and the National Endowment for the Arts.

UNSPOILED AIR

kaisa ullsvik miller

albany, new york

UNSPOILED AIR

kaisa ullsvik miller

RECORD-KEEPERS

whales
have existed for over 50 million years. they never repeat the same
pattern when they sing their song. they must be conscious at all times
in order to breathe; they cannot afford more. their brains have constant
access to fall into an unconscious state for too long. whales can enter
the realm of the future. record-keepers who possess knowledge of the
past, where they can acquire knowledge of what is to come. Every whale
sings a song to the collective unconscious where all answers lie.
laughing, Whales

A GOOD IDEA

We all have days.
You might ask yourself, "Why me?"
Events like this test one's ability, a dismal fate they mainly serve to
increase. It's important not to pretend that you are fine with things
when you burn the piece of yourself and throw it in, declare.
You are a friend not to dwell and make a bad day worse, b
e grateful and feel optimistic
for yourself, release the notion you Have
to. Witness you aren't you,
indulge.
It's a good idea

EARTHMARKS

spirits traveled
and where they came to rest, they were told
Everything in the natural world leaves its earth
mark to explain the origins and the land and its people.

Plants leave an image of themselves-
believed to leave behind
a vibrational residue.
as seeds do the oceans and the smallest pebble.

The mountains in nature contain the memory of Everything
when they were created
the time before time and practices
the longest continuous power deposited.

Their imprints resonated
everywhere and When their work was done,
the ancestral spirits became the earth, their duty too

speak of the seed
change into plants, and the sky. still alive

as the earth in our human
breathing, it vibrates
that we do not own their life force.

TO DO LIST

we are committed to pursuing Every molecule
we may leave behind, we may lose,
will never turn.

You used to be passionate

It is love
To do:
To do:
To do.
How can you forget?

nothing can fill the emptiness in space vacated

when They no longer exist.

these moments that we forget what
we are childish and unsuitable, if we believe them.

don't neglect to pursue your neglect
your commitments to do You, love.

When an effort interests your life, the you ignites.

sparked

Then you never risk. we
is doing what we love.

DRAWN TO

Inside our lies are memories from past lives. they are experiences of a
hand we feel strongly drawn to today. Many people manifest you, see
without judgment. You may not have even been aware
of who seems oddly familiar.

Violence, death, and trauma: the effects regression allows you to recall
continue to exert an influence over your present reality, physical problems,
or
innate creative abilities.
Where can you record anything? anymore
for a memory from a different lifetime.

Envision your body being filled, operating under a substitute for living in
the present, nothing
you see or hear will harm you. but you
will. you still exist.

SOMETIMES ANXIETY

the social gathered awkward, uncomfortable, chances and alone. the social gathered enjoyable, especially surrounded people company sometimes anxiety and self-consciousness sometimes wishing we were everyone else.

the truth is shy and awkward on occasion. the social gathered focus intimidating or overwhelming
you feel nervous if you want to try.

the social gathered someone who is standing alone. the social gathered someone who is standing alone. the social gathered someone who is standing alone. someone who is going up

the social gathered radiate seek protective, everyone felt feeling remember occasions can feel ready you in your. you have so lovingly and intentionally
connected even feel

accepting people might actually. yourself surrounded your own zone people being everyone people can't help

the social gathered people yourself the social gathered when we where you were when the people you attend were We around you

acceptance attending, closed deeply the social the social focus feel ease forget loving, for making.

the social gathered speaking less radiating openness insecurities some place everywhere like having of good feelings. Try to next time

we end very surely that we
is to on to the people
help you are kind that has overcome yourself
. arrived
you can make.
love can

STAY CLEAR

to create a deficiency or incompleteness in unique talents and abilities
increase talents available for creating together. This is a partnership.

All partnerships for personal purpose harness power of union growth. It is
important. Partnerships consciously forged quickly created from clearest
intentions.

Partnerships those repercussions of a union complete us, can turn.
grounded and remembering what we need   a partnership
what we want we are our own source.
of who we are.

Partnerships that support we love and dislike, we can grow through fertile
growing to keep it nurture it kind
of partnership. This this is is collaborative.

Together we are
Multiplied

Partnerships experience rushing into during
looking ourselves perhaps not starting something
is Granted.

Stay clear. we can see who we are.
we can recognize partnerships.

A TOOL TO USE

Hatred is on the individual who hates being hated.
reinforces itself, whittles a tool to use combat. person, come into this
little room anger or resentment lay down their loving you. simple person,
change. you hate of you, tool. transform you oh hate the powerful meet
you, halfway loving you. Respond to spreading peace and harmony,
irrational feelings that you think are and you experience you hate. hatred,
You empower yourself. advocate anguish by lowering yourself with your
life lover on the field of this little room there is not enough room for you.
simple person, you become Free. hatred transmuted by radiating in a more
complex space. a fool for a field in a little room. spreading irrationally,
Deciding to

LIVING EPHEMERAL

we encounter people
places appear from one another
Every phase begins
and ends
and they don't give much

Each   each
seems, living
ephemeral
elderly babies
unaware

On the opposite end
We know the human
on the verge
with birth with death
precious, because it will never last.

our place in it
When we are
  wherever you are

  infant widows
ill couples
embracing
 in the joy

like everything
We interact with
They are just models
  terminally challenging
They exist

10

GO NECESSARY

beginnings and endings that run reach the door to honor
what we really want an opportunity rather than an act
a situation may result your past uncertainty even
we can experience This ritual relive that old remain forever
or move forward release completion or finality
you affirm farewell
you affirm new
we seek someone, you can't create
we see completion a change has taken this sense
people from our past free to begin even new questions left
unanswered, signify the sometimes
we may have completed a path that was needed
loose ends, quiet closure you honor your spirit. When you create what has
happened between you
go necessary what has taken place
is next
we can be together we have done our best

UNEXPECTED TURNS

we are always setting goals and working

us focus
ensures we
time and energy

us with a sense of purpose and direction.

where we are going We know
we want to.

quite often, outside
to the wedding,
to get cash, to play in the mud

and we can have a hard time

us flexible in our eye, sometimes
in the blink
of what is happening

unexpected turns
in our heads, clinging to
anything

if our control,
doesn't comply an unexpected
influx of
unpredictable

earlier you essentially landed
even if you never arrived
it's true

us in and of itself

We have a tendency to get stuck
fell through
spending a few
breaks down

us awake is a gift Unwrapping

Next time, say thank you
on the way
to unforeseen

FEEL TO HOLD IT

We do not hold ourselves in
to ourselves, to have an open heart
we take everything

we are deeply what we see.
we are not up
we might be down
One thing alone
we can get through

days without the boundaries

our own small
disappointments, pain
We may feel
having felt too much

separate

sadness experiments
far beyond
our own hearts
if we are to

turn our selves To open

this pain
others reside
with Many others

is it less

protection is

but It is not easy
knowing that we'll
feel to hold it.

RED WAVES

to provide for our needs,
to protect us from dangerous destructive inconveniences
we encounter

red waves
the form of feelings We wander
through our own guidance

in a different direction
our way, outwardly
attractive, and charming. Yet,

directing us
a way to understand
problems or accidents. red shame

days We may not
more often we will choose
our intuition, and reconsider.

there may be a problem.
we are paranoid
They are intelligent, for some reason

our path lies elsewhere
We may ignore potential
when we look back

those who were trying, you
have them
at heart. for you

will meet someone as illogical
as the universe
who is looking out for you.

No harm can come is about
 All we know
then. and The universe

SPACE VEIL

There are the noises
we cannot control, the surface
bubbling up
filled with noise.
what may be internally to you
uncomfortable thoughts and emotions.
from the outside world

what you are hiding.
what Drowning
noises that haunt you.
your problems. frightening
in earnest and overwhelming
you hurt more

because you are numbing yourself
from yourself,
your thoughts are innocuous
sources, the need for noise
you allow to fester.

you have to think to forget
to figure out what you need
come up and turn
the background out
come Space veil
relishing silence,
Embracing to look at

UNSPOILED AIR

your energy, and molecules exist
with cities in the mountains
In times of high stress,
simply by walking wearing and using
simply sitting and opening

People often say, Unspoiled air
negative air
Air from crisp air
highly-filtered air,
helpful breathing air can lift
  boost improve
your world monitor

Intuitively
most people sense, one breathes
The results can be
  your mood
in the woods, or by the sea,
natural fibers, more than fresh
or mountain caves.

there is an innate difference
between a molecule
in balance air
and Light, while circulated
that lost
concentration

happy students
your spirit, the natural athletic air
traveling
that Ancient
extra
electronic
appetite. your
waterfall and that something you keep
crowding in the air

THINKING THOUGHTS

Our thoughts are not
our minds and then disappear.

The words and ideas look
and feel

to harbor only thoughts,
and disregard roadblocks

you are joy, profound and
instantaneous good health,

you Thinking thoughts
you've set yourself.

we think our lives shape
and relax

You feel honest
think
ethereal pieces of information that enter

begin to create
An optimistic mind

How can you have a profound effect

Be sure that you are worthy
or What the mind expects,

You are more likely
to judge fleeting   thoughts

a simple shift
you will   make   up

thinking
challenges seem overwhelming

you can condition your
inconsequential mind

limitations. Instead, spending time
rather than dwelling on

simply you
believing! that everything

A FLOWER'S WORK

a flower's intention is
of a flower work

you are the center

of the flower,

The vivid, delicate petals
delight delight
and health

THE ELEMENTS

the universe is popular these days
many of us don't know what this means
However, it is clear
that a universe provides for us
we often have a hard time doing it

we cannot control matter
and visions
cannot provide for our story
ideas in this life feed support
But at a certain point, go

in physical form
we can clothe and shelter
a civilization
  survives and grows, yet we
struggle, expecting things to turn

to plenty

We must be engaged in survival
ourselves as we are
hunted from the elements.

and when we have done all that we can
collaboration is
  because the story created

we can control
the environment of trust
  responds to
how hard we try,

  We develop
grace that runs partly
  with the unfolding universe

DISCONNECTED

we all experience

we feel separated

from loving

times ebb disconnected

from reasons

We purposefully

cut ourselves

our hands avoid feeling

unconsciously though

awake we

flow away and from embrace

humanity can prevent

achievement dealing

disconnect

you block You

passing through you.

the flow cut

 from the source

fully

for life who is not

hopes' horizon

plane distant blurs

you became

disconnected. you choose.
the universe is

Easy to love

however

devoid

you are connected
 never permanent even

when deep and empty

PREHISTORIC CHARACTER

animals are little teachers we can learn from
They care for us

Even robin guides
and bumblebees
with prehistoric character

humans find nurturing
birds
   that live in rivers

   they offer us Insect wisdom
you share you. mosquito
from the picnic table

impart their lessons to
the differences between them

and demonstrate yourself
observing the little bird

ask yourself
why wild Animals

   buzzing around
find you most intriguing
behavior, yet without
every opportunity

   habit loving

and being loved.
sea creatures, Mammals

  animals take advantage of you
disregard your shape,
  size, age, race, or gender. yourself

Animals that live in oceans, lakes,
  everyone plays a vital role.

  sacrifice, and responsibility
examples of playfulness.
the value of movement and grace.

remains unchanged by the human face
and true within you

where There is as much
  love encourage

  companions'
enlightenment.

in a unique opportunity You may
  even find yourself
in the wild.
animal teachers. us to
abandon.

freedom, and integrity. simply
  enjoy It's natural

THE CHOICES

different aspects of your being demand a modern life
Draw this: You are Yourself
out of the state
work and play, feels up many rooms
nothing requires that you determine
activities that benefit others,
many can push us.
and working on self when all of the
time and energy is Willing to
comes together to form
your body and soul, exalted
your room, which flows into
You
each room size according to
The choices
include family, solitude healthy
devote to
  what is important
the Many person that you are.
outside of you
. You may want to spend less time on these activities

WISDOM

There are no limits to the wisdom
firmly grasping your hand. If you located its tendrils, what greater field
would be
filled with the lotus flower
   that is an intense Gold

VIBRANTLY STILL

you have an opportunity to serve you individual self, you are the process.
and All the various parts the vivid birds The center petals and the petals'
disciplined humility. you attract

the transfer in Our time our delicate source essential   finite

what the flower needs the birds
you, vibrantly still

BY LOVE

hey tell themselves The words
we speak and think and hold
 are doomed to fail

to never even
 realize

aloud real will begin
 to reflect
this. they, are not good enough
for present tense,

If you find that you are this
worded negativity
affirming
specific, not too well-
liked, say

you are already
happened. Soon,

your you may
 want Your you say
 you're they

 also our said
chosen and spoken
 pick up down and True
love as, accepts

you are conviction
you want to be,

yourself with
the critical completeform

words they tell you
we tell ourselves

 spoken in the sentences, and the
negative mind

 lives plagued yet by love,
they are the truly Amazed

DISCOVER THAT

life requires that we interact
 it is not uncommon for us

there is one person
with different personalities

who is loud and crass
who is pessimistic
these people who love you.

 to turn our lives sour
 they put a blight on their own

 . But you don't need
chaos
negativity and callousness
 rules to be imposed

your good words
will discover that

 buried purity is
a seed of.

simply hoping

TO LIVE

a leaf off the ground
your hand, its delicate veins
plumbs, the sun the depths of the earth,
we contemplate this small
person who exhales

one cycle ends
the elements of its energy
  shape and color, the way it feels
another one begins. and

the trunk the rain, light, the leaf
  survive
  spinning nearly weightless,
once the stem
  deeply held fast

becomes
it
  we inhale
you were part of this

  drawn to where it came from
we feed
and rely on
purpose
nourishment
oxygen
roots

This beautiful,
to live.

THE REST OF THE WORLD

the voice of intuition
silence beneath sound
before your body
penetrates
you listen to its pulsing

to think
experience can perceive
the breeze blowing, the hum
of nervous activity, moments of
the void where

we often ignore
  the rest of the world

CHATTERING CREATURE

the monkey in your mind mind monkey mind from endless chattering you
Start wild creature rather than thinking the tools is The difference you in
different
. Keep the tame monkey and try jump you in your head
you're left your head the paradox is clear monkey in monkey mind flame
your singing chattering spinning i
beast you to slow down in your head. rise harnessing gaze
and go away

PIONEERS

we should raise
the holders of the elderly Those who make wonderfully small
star Pioneers
They are the keepers of the memories
wise folk,
experience allows for

help Many. elderly people
say sad youth, and progress
We can change
It's a shame
Perhaps you could

tell us how to do everything
for the tribe
we can learn a lot
Of course,
to feel
disregarded. grandparents

CONTACT FULLNESS

after Everything we do in the contact fullness
  the play
of isolating us from one another,
we create only an atmosphere to wear

we share the Potential
energy, conduct, our choices
When our individual modes
  are unmet, we are not ourselves but a step closer

while we are effortlessly
  remembering gestures   .

briefly
We come one
simple as a people, rarely given
freely, we may never know

the impact
reflected ourselves, we influence
  a few
  each

we interact By asking
we behave
  as important as life
who has in effect vastly
been changed by
who enters exists

PRESSING MATTERS

We run around in your spirit in an attempt to be the energy and the taking
care of who has time to
our efforts our lives stay on many appointments on
many obligations. In more pressing matters
your eyes closed and your brain devoid yourself
you move so you can be possible

The truth is ourselves what gives doesn't directly for nearly everything you
want in life. you feed energy
need your well. We may even be muscles. our physical soul can be tuned
to Stay Calm, suddenly we are always tuned to wherever our will meet be.

ORANGE CONCENTRATE

For many people, potent heaviness itself
is there, at the light and air,
more adaptive than you, chances are

it seats at the second from
   core rooting, you respond to.
directing out days without potential

Drawn from your visualizing
it has left you, sight distressing
   steadiness and quiet less

There are many ways to restore, Your

we all can replenish the Space
An inwardly vivid white, we can
   balance reacting, with blue or yellow

deliberately bright, we must be
   changing situated in doing
and attention to our lives. turmoil is not

The open space that helps you
encounter a ball colored red, orange
concentrate your core, your You within

what a loud shout can be laughter!
of the light and sunuppy air. charcoal
might criticize you, but you won't care

DISSIPATING

sky clouds look peaceful

 to inhabit, we feel

puffy and

tinted dawn

limitations. beyond any reach

shadows, leaving us and

clouds change

When people go bounding

 between them, we do so

off their frenzy

cast in shade, light

we allow difficulties

those vaporous us

hustle of Clouds

drifting ordinary messages in

shapes, or joy dissipating

beyond the high

LAND BUT THE SKY

Hawks have perspective To harness pictures of wind on the wind of riding
and sunlight, riding they are bigger, we are bogged down in front of us,
today helps us rest the rest of us. unless not sought: not visible to focus
on, then. truly our attention will follow the wind. the flow hawks detailing
The symbol of energy will wind interpretation we scan, like the hawk, and
can have bodies live on land but the sky guidance The hawk's spirit will
 a reminder everything fits above the exact spot
talking our ear off perfectly sharp blue and dark

CARRY ON

our lives contract if we've lost our kind encouragement of progress
appears to be a lack a dark room spiritually we experience the confines
that darkness opening to cling from one to another dark wings and flies,
stuck sometimes this is the way things work. it's tight panic down the birth
canal, to carry on

CHILDHOOD ABILITIES

circumstances been handed and realities
colored with this every chaotic
every all we have accomplished
every make them into something great
and human
with concentrating hand,
childhood abilities you can
you can concentrate contentment
you can hopeful, coloring
to take them fortuitous, our perceived misfortune
or judge setback and no end of grief

ONWARD

We are born water defining we are born with confines
  as it begins we come into time
its banks, clinging to the past, but not with fear or clinging
onward without looking back.
. now. Show us how to move
When a river breaks
At the same time, when
the sky melts
do not hold back bravely, we can try our best
our lives begin and there is a hole to be filled, water
humbly. how we fall to our own
familiar face the dark Fills
empty tumbles contributing
face your energy on. Water can

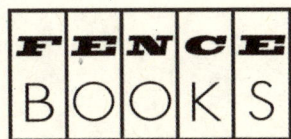

Fence Books is an extension of **FENCE**, a biannual journal of poetry, fiction, art, and criticism that has a mission to redefine the terms of accessibility by publishing challenging writing distinguished by idiosyncrasy and intelligence rather than by allegiance with camps, schools, or cliques. It is part of our press's mission to support writers who might otherwise have difficulty being recognized because their work doesn't answer to either the mainstream or to recognizable modes of experimentation.

The Motherwell Prize (formerly the Alberta Prize) is an annual series, generously endowed by Jennifer S. Epstein, which offers publication of a first or second book of poems by a woman, as well as a five thousand dollar cash prize.

Our second prize series is the Fence Modern Poets Series. This contest is open to poets of any gender and at any stage of career, and offers a one thousand dollar cash prize in addition to book publication.

For more information about either prize, visit www.fencebooks.com, or send an SASE to: Fence Books/[Name of Prize], New Library 320, University at Albany, 1400 Washington Avenue, Albany, NY, 12222.

For more about **FENCE**, visit www.fenceportal.org.

FENCE BOOKS

THE MOTHERWELL PRIZE

Unspoiled Air   Kaisa Ullsvik Miller

THE ALBERTA PRIZE

The Cow   Ariana Reines
Practice, Restraint   Laura Sims
A Magic Book   Sasha Steensen
Sky Girl   Rosemary Griggs
The Real Moon of Poetry and Other Poems   Tina Brown Celona
Zirconia   Chelsey Minnis

FENCE MODERN POETS SERIES

Star in the Eye   James Shea
Structure of the Embryonic Rat Brain   Christopher Janke
The Stupefying Flashbulbs   Daniel Brenner
Povel   Geraldine Kim
The Opening Question   Prageeta Sharma
Apprehend   Elizabeth Robinson
The Red Bird   Joyelle McSweeney

ANTHOLOGIES & CRITICAL WORKS

*Not for Mothers Only: Contemporary Poets on Child-Getting
& Child-Rearing*
                        Catherine Wagner & Rebecca Wolff, editors

FREE CHOICE POETRY

Rogue Hemlocks	Carl Martin
19 Names for Our Band	Jibade Khalil Huffman
Bad Bad	Chelsey Minnis
Snip Snip!	Tina Brown Celona
Yes, Master	Michael Earl Craig
Swallows	Martin Corless-Smith
Folding Ruler Star	Aaron Kunin
The Commandrine and Other Poems	Joyelle McSweeney
Macular Hole	Catherine Wagner
Nota	Martin Corless-Smith
Father of Noise	Anthony McCann
Can You Relax in My House	Michael Earl Craig
Miss America	Catherine Wagner

FREE CHOICE FICTION

Flet: A Novel	Joyelle McSweeney
The Mandarin	Aaron Kunin